Ducklings Grow Up

by Victoria Torres

I need to know these words.

duck

ducklings

eggs

swim

Look at this mother duck.

This mother duck has some eggs.

Look at the eggs.

Little ducklings are in the eggs.

The ducklings are coming out!

The mother duck has
little ducklings.
The ducklings can sleep.

The ducklings can eat.

The ducklings can walk, too.
The ducklings walk in the grass.

The ducklings swim.
They swim in the water.
The ducklings swim
with their mother.

The ducklings get bigger
and bigger.

Look!

The ducklings are ducks now.